WINNING KEYS IN TROUBLED TIMES

LEKE SANUSI

Copyright (c) 2012 by Leke Sanusi

Published by ORAWORD PUBLISHERS LTD
146 Iron Mill Lane
Crayford
Kent
DA1 4RX
United Kingdom

Website: www.lekesanusi.com
e-mail: lekesanusi@aol.com;
lekesanusi@rccgvictoryhouse.com
Tel: 0207 252 7522

ISBN: 978-0-9854723-1-3

Unless otherwise stated, scripture quotations are taken from the King James Version of the Holy bible.

Printed by supremeprinters.com

DEDICATION

I dedicate this book to you, my beloved reader. I welcome you to your season of Jubilee and I hereby decree into manifestation your five-fold Jubilee blessings: Restoration, Release, Rest, Recovery and Rejoice!

Rejoice. Again, I say Rejoice in the Lord. It is your JUBILEE!

ACKNOWLEDGEMENT

I give all glory, praises and thanks to the Almighty God for His unfailing love to me before and since I came to this world. I am eternally grateful to my Lord Jesus Christ for saving my soul, taking me out of the miry clay, planting my feet upon the rock, establishing my goings and giving me a new song. I pray many shall see the song of salvation through me and fear You, O God.

I thank all my families, friends, colleagues, co-workers, associates, teachers, parishioners, prayer partners and indeed all whose paths I have had to cross in this journey so far. I thank you for allowing God to use you as my helpers of destiny in one way or the other. I pray that you will forever enjoy divine help in Jesus name.

"When things go wrong as they sometimes will
When the road you're trudging seems all up hill
When the funds are low and the debts are high
And you want to smile, but you have to sigh,
And care is pressing you down a bit,
Rest if you must, but don't you quit.
Life is queer with its twists and turns,
As every one of us sometimes learns,
And many a failure turns about
When he might have won had he stuck it out;
Don't give up though the pace seems slow,
You may succeed with another blow,
Success is failure turned inside out.
The silver tint of the clouds of doubt,
And you never can tell how close you are,
It may be near when it seems so far;
So stick to the fight when you are hardest hit,
It's when things seem worst that you must not quit."
-Unknown

CONTENTS

INTRODUCTION

17 Although the fig tree shall not blossom, neither shall fruit be in the vines; the labour of the olive shall fail, and the fields shall yield no meat; the flock shall be cut off from the fold, and there shall be no herd in the stalls: 18 Yet I will rejoice in the LORD, I will joy in the God of my salvation. 19 The LORD God is my strength, and he will make my feet like hinds' feet, and he will make me to walk upon mine high places.

Hab. 3:17-19 (KJV)

17 Even though the fig trees have no blossoms, and there are no grapes on the vines; even though the olive crop fails, and the fields lie empty and barren; even though the flocks die in the fields, and the cattle barns are empty,18 yet I will rejoice in the LORD! I will be joyful in the God of my salvation!19 The Sovereign LORD is my strength! He makes me as surefooted as a deer, able to tread upon the heights.

Hab. 3:17-19 (NLT)

The above is a powerful scripture answering many questions such as, will you praise God even when things are not going right or the way you expect? Just like in the days of the prophet Habakkuk who penned down the above, we are living in troubled times. These are troubled times spiritually, economically, politically, socially etc. The whole world is living in troubled times. *"...and the whole world lieth in wickedness" 1John.5:19*

People are troubled everywhere. Experts are foretelling woes and crisis. There is political unrest all over the world like never before. Economic recession and depression have gripped the entire hemisphere. We hear of wars and rumours of war everywhere. People are jobless and those who have are losing or on the verge of losing their jobs. Homeowners face repossession or the threat of it. Families are troubled. Marriages are scattering. There is health crisis all over the world.

These happened in the days of Prophet Habakkuk. Olive crops were failing to grow; the fig tree was not blossoming; flocks were dying in the field and the cattle barns were empty. In spite of it all, the prophet said he will still praise God because it was God who created him and the God of salvation will deliver him.

For many of us and may be you, the reader of this book, your fig tree may not be blossoming. Your career has nose dived; there is sickness in the body; your expectations are being cut short; output is not matching input; many things are not working well for you. You may even be coming out of a season of fasting and prayer now. Heavens seem shut. God appears so far away. You see emptiness everywhere you turn.

It may be that the flocks are dying meaning that you have suffered losses here and there. It could be loss of material things; the loss of a job or a loved one; the loss of investment or an opportunity. It may also be the loss of a marriage or the prospect of losing one. Prophet Habakkuk said he will still be glad and rejoice in all these trials and tribulations. He teaches us that God has not changed and He would not change from being a faithful God and Saviour who is able to save and deliver from whatever trial and trouble we are going through. *"For I am the Lord, I change not..."* *Mal.3:6.*

Troubled times are real. What we are going through in these days and times cannot be covered with the veil of religiosity. The pain and pangs are real. The losses and lapses are real. The deprivations and depravities are real. The recession and regression are real. The plagues and poverty are real; the setbacks and sufferings are real; the bankruptcy and barrenness are real. So real also is our GOD. God the Helper of the helpless is real. God the generous Giver is real; God the proven Provider is real. God the winning Warrior is real; God the heavenly Healer is real; God the constant Comforter is real; God the Silencer of storms is real. God the faithful Friend is real. This 'Omni-Positive' Reality called God is more than sufficient to cancel all the negative realities. Praise God!

1 But now the Lord who created you, O Israel, says, "Don't be afraid, for I have ransomed you; I have called you by name; you are mine. 2 When you go through deep waters and great trouble, I will be with you. When you go through rivers of difficulty, you will not drown! When you walk through the fire of oppression, you will not be burned up—the flames will not consume you. 3 For I am the Lord your God, your Savior, the Holy One of Israel. I gave Egypt and Ethiopia and Seba [to Cyrus] in exchange for your freedom, as your ransom. Isaiah 43:1-3 (TLB)

As real as our troubled times are, God the Troubler of troubles is even more real. The Solver, the Deliverer, the Way-Maker; the One who is able to turn the captivity; the One that makes a way where there seems to be no way is also real. When that mountain confronts you in the face, you too must confront the mountain and say to it "My mountain mover is real". That is what the prophet Habakkuk affirmed by saying in effect: *Though there may be problems, yet I will rejoice because I know when I do that, God will give me strength. He will make my feet as strong as the deer and will give me the speed to run, to overtake and overcome the mountains.*

6 Then he answered and spake unto me, saying, This is the word of the LORD unto Zerubbabel, saying, Not by might, nor by power, but by my spirit, saith the LORD of hosts. 7 Who art thou, O great mountain? before Zerubbabel thou shalt become a plain: and he shall bring forth

the headstone thereof with shoutings, crying,
Grace, grace unto it. Zech 4:6-7 (KJV)

There are keys to open the door of breakthroughs in troubled times such as the world is in right now. Those keys are expressed in terms of the right attitudes that will guarantee survival and revival. The following chapters explain the keys. Read; reflect on and release these attitudinal keys and you will be walking on the winning way.

KEY ONE

RECOGNIZE PURPOSE IN PROBLEMS

17 Although the fig tree shall not blossom, neither shall fruit be in the vines; the labour of the olive shall fail, and the fields shall yield no meat; the flock shall be cut off from the fold, and there shall be no herd in the stalls: 18 Yet I will rejoice in the LORD, I will joy in the God of my salvation. 19 The LORD God is my strength, and he will make my feet like hinds' feet, and he will make me to walk upon mine high places. Hab 3:17-19 (KJV)

5 Behold ye among the heathen, and regard, and wonder marvellously: for I will work a work in your days, which ye will not believe, though it be told you. Hab 1:5 (KJV)

The first winning key in troubled times is to recognize that there is a purpose in every problem that confronts a child of God in particular. A man had a problem. He was troubled with blindness from birth. One day, Jesus Christ and his disciples were passing by and the latter asked Jesus who sinned that the man was born blind. The Lord's reply is worthy of note: *"..Neither hath this man sinned nor his parents: but that the works of God should be made manifest in him" Jn.9:3.* In effect, there was a divine purpose in his problem. In the same way, I make bold to say that whatever trouble you are going through right now has a divine purpose in it that is waiting to be revealed.

Joni Eareckson Tada said: *"It is a glorious thing to know that your Father God makes no mistakes in directing or permitting that which crosses the path of your life. It is the glory of God to conceal a matter. It is our glory to trust Him, no matter what."*

1 To every thing there is a season, and a time to every purpose under the heaven: Eccl 3:1 (KJV)

28 And we know that all things work together for good to them that love God, to them who are the called according to his purpose. Romans 8:28 (KJV)

Pray Now:

1. *Father, give me deep spiritual insight into what I am going through right now in the name of Jesus.*
2. *Father, open the eyes of my understanding and enlighten my darkness in the name of Jesus.*
3. *Holy Spirit, help me to look beyond my present circumstances and alert me to your divine plan and purpose in the name of Jesus.*
4. *Father, command my negative situations to begin to work together for my good in the name of Jesus.*
5. *O Lord, give me understanding of the times and teach me what to do in the name of Jesus.*
6. *Father, blind my vision to the pain but open my eyes to the gain in my problem in the name of Jesus.*

In Genesis.37-50. Joseph suffered all manners of troubled times in the hands of his own brothers. They envied and hated him for his dreams. They conspired against him. They threw him into the pit. They pronounced death sentence against him and announced his obituary to his father. They sold him to slavery and that also led to many other troubles. One day his dream came to pass, his brothers appeared before him and bowed! This year, your enemies will bow to you in the name of Jesus. While Joseph's brothers feared reprisal from their brother whom they condemned to afflictions years ago, they must have been shocked by the way Joseph perceived the entire experience: Here is what transpired:

16 And they sent a messenger unto Joseph, saying, Thy father did command before he died, saying, 17 So shall ye say unto Joseph, Forgive, I pray thee now, the trespass of thy brethren, and their sin; for they did unto thee evil: and now, we pray thee, forgive the trespass of the servants of the God of thy father. And Joseph wept when they spake unto him. 18 And his brethren also went and fell down before his face; and they said, Behold, we be thy servants. 19 And Joseph said unto them, Fear not: for am I in the place of God? 20 But as for you, ye thought evil against me; but God meant it unto

*good, to bring to pass, as it is this day, to save
much people alive. 21 Now therefore fear ye
not: I will nourish you, and your little ones. And
he comforted them, and spake kindly unto them.
Gen 50:16-21 (KJV)*

Joseph saw purpose in problem. This is why it is not
good to repay evil for evil. It is ungodly to hate even
those who hate you.

Jesus Christ said: *27 But I say unto you which
hear, Love your enemies, do good to them
which hate you, 28 Bless them that curse you,
and pray for them which despitefully use you.
29 And unto him that smiteth thee on the one
cheek offer also the other; and him that taketh
away thy cloke forbid not to take thy coat
also. Luke 6:27-29 (KJV)
14 Bless them which persecute you: bless, and
curse not. Romans 12:14 (KJV)*

If you understand the purpose of God, it may well be
that you will end up thanking those who hated and
persecuted you because without them, you may not
experience divine breakthroughs and fulfil your
destiny. If they had not conspired to throw the three

Hebrew men into the fiery furnace, their promotion in a foreign land might not have been possible. This year, God will use your detractors to attract favour and promotion to you in Jesus' name. Pray the following prayers aloud!

7. *Father, give me the grace to love those who hate me and never to repay evil with evil in the name of Jesus.*

8. *O Lord, let the expectations of the wicked concerning me be disappointed and frustrated in the name of Jesus.*

9. *This year, I shall see everything turning around in my favour in the name of Jesus.*

10. *Let every wicked counsel be turned around for God's divine purpose for my life in the name of Jesus.*

11. *Lord, my times are in your hands, deliver me from my persecutors in the name of Jesus.*

12. *Father, in everything, help me to maintain a thankful and grateful attitude in the name of Jesus.*

13. *Father, let my enemies make the mistake that will advance my cause in the name of Jesus.*

14. *Father, disappoint the devices of the wicked concerning me and frustrate their expectations in the name of Jesus.*

15. *Every seed of bitterness, unforgiveness and hurt,*

be uprooted and destroyed from my life in the name of Jesus.

16. *Let every counsel of the wicked against my destiny be turned to foolishness in the mighty name of Jesus.*

17. *Lord Jesus, help me and give me the grace to walk in Your steps.*

God allowed His only begotten son, Jesus Christ to suffer afflictions and endure troubled times because He had a work to do and a purpose to accomplish. The salvation of mankind was primary to God and the suffering of Christ became secondary to Him.

16 For God so loved the world, that he gave his only begotten Son, that whosoever believeth in him should not perish, but have everlasting life. 17 For God sent not his Son into the world to condemn the world; but that the world through him might be saved. John 3:15-17 (KJV)

God's purpose was accomplished as His son submitted to His will and learned obedience by the things which he suffered. Satan, who had hoped to benefit from the crucifixion of the Saviour, is now regretting what he did. If he had known that crucifixion would pave way for the salvation of man, he would have left the Son of God alone.

> *8 Which none of the princes of this world knew: for had they known it, they would not have crucified the Lord of glory. 9 But as it is written, Eye hath not seen, nor ear heard, neither have entered into the heart of man, the things which God hath prepared for them that love him. 1.Cor 2:8-9 (KJV)*

18. *Father, command the stumbling blocks of my adversaries to become stepping stones to my breakthroughs in the name of Jesus.*
19. *Lord, let whatever I am going through be for your ultimate glory in the name of Jesus.*
20. *Father, open my eyes to see your invisible divine purpose for my destiny in the name of Jesus.*
21. *Every power assigned to defeat God's purpose for my life, scatter in the mighty name of Jesus.*
22. *Father, light shines the best in the worst of darkness, let my light arise in the midst of my present afflictions and begin to shine brightest in Jesus' name.*

23. *Father, this year, give me an Ephraim miracle and make me fruitful in the land of my affliction in the name of Jesus.*

With God, delay is no denial; waiting is no wastage. God has a perfect timing for those who wait on.

11 He hath made every thing beautiful in his time: also he hath set the world in their heart, so that no man can find out the work that God maketh from the beginning to the end. Eccl 3:11 (KJV)

2 My brethren, count it all joy when ye fall into divers temptations; 3 Knowing this, that the trying of your faith worketh patience. 4 But let patience have her perfect work, that ye may be perfect and entire, wanting nothing. James 1:2-4 (KJV)

If you trust God completely, the trials you are going through now will end in triumph and you will be thanking God you went through the trials. The bible says in Rom.8:28: *28 And we know that all things work together for good to them that love God, to them who are the called according to his purpose.*

John Henry Newman said *"I will trust Him. Whatever, wherever I am, I can never be thrown away. If I am in sickness, my sickness may serve Him; in perplexity, my perplexity may serve Him; if I am in sorrow, my sorrow may serve Him. My sickness, or perplexity, or sorrow may be necessary causes of some great end, which is quite beyond us. He does nothing in vain".*

It was a very trying period for my wife and I as we experienced delayed childbearing for many years. Today, how wonderful has the Lord allowed that trial to shape our destinies. I probably would not be saved from the greater tribulation of hell if I had not gone through that trial. The delay became the pathway to destiny. That will be your testimony this year in Jesus name. Pray now.

24. *Father, give me the grace to rejoice in hope and be patient in tribulation in the name of Jesus.*

25. *I confess that the joy of the Lord is my strength in the name of Jesus.*

26. *Father, let me live to declare your glory, your work and your purpose in the land of the living in the name of Jesus.*

27. *Father, after this trying period let me come forth as gold in the name of Jesus.*

28. *Father, use my present wilderness experience to prepare me for your wonderful divine assignment for me in the mighty name of Jesus.*

29. *I command the storms around me to pass away that the glory of the Lord might be revealed in the name of Jesus.*

30. *Powers that have vowed to truncate my destiny, you are liars, I shall laugh last in the name of Jesus.*

31. *Father, let every step I take from now on and every move I make from now on lead to the fulfilment of your purpose for my life in the name of Jesus.*

RECOGNIZE PURPOSE IN PROBLEMS: It is a winning key in troubled times.

KEY TWO

REMEMBER HIS PAST MERCIES

⁹ [Zion now cries to the Lord, the God of Israel] Awake, awake, put on strength and might, O arm of the Lord; awake, as in the ancient days, as in the generations of long ago. Was it not You Who cut Rahab [Egypt] in pieces, Who pierced the dragon [symbol of Egypt]? ¹⁰ Was it not You Who dried up the Red Sea, the waters of the great deep, Who made the depths of the sea a way for the redeemed to pass over? [Why then are we left so long in captivity?] ¹¹ [The Lord God says] And the redeemed of the Lord shall return and come with singing to Zion; everlasting joy shall be upon their heads. They

shall obtain joy and gladness, and sorrow and
sighing shall flee away. Isaiah 51:9-11 (AMP)

In troubled times, you must remember God's past mercies and that should strengthen you to survive the storm. In the above story, the children of Israel were facing troubled times in captivity. They have been there for a long time and weariness was setting in. In crying to the Lord for deliverance, they remembered that He had delivered them from the hands of strong foes before. They recounted how He delivered them from Egypt, how God made a way for His people in the red sea, where there seemed to be no way. They confessed and acknowledged God's display of His power in the days of old. Their testimony moved God. That is why it is always good to share testimonies of what God has done for you.

God responded to their acknowledgment of His past mercies by assuring them of deliverance this time again. *"And the redeemed of the Lord shall return and come with singing......"*
    ⁶ Remember, O Lord, Your tender mercy and loving-kindness; for they have been ever from of old. Psalms 25:6 (AMP)

God has not changed. He is the same yesterday and today and forever (Heb.13:8) What He has done before, He can do it again. Whatever you are going through, remember with thanksgiving God's past mercies and he will be moved in your favour again this time.

1. *Father, I remember with thanksgiving your past mercies over my life.*
2. *It is of your mercies that I am not consumed. Your compassions fail not.*
3. *I thank You Lord for seeing me through in the journey of life up until now.*
4. *Father, truly You have been faithful even when I was not faithful.*
5. *Whatever I am today Lord, it is by Your grace. All glory to You in the name of Jesus.*
6. *From the time of my conception in the womb till now, Your mercy has kept me. I praise Your Holy name.*

37 David said moreover, The LORD that delivered me out of the paw of the lion, and out of the paw of the bear, he will deliver me out of the hand of this Philistine. And Saul said unto David, Go, and the LORD be with thee. 1 Sam 17:37 (KJV)

David's confidence was boosted by the unfailing power of God which he experienced when wild animals attacked him. He concluded that this same God will deliver him from the present 'beast' of a Goliath confronting him.

Has the Lord delivered you from anything before? May be you are thinking and saying 'am not sure'. I can help you to be sure. He has indeed delivered you from several things that would have made you either a nonentity or a forgotten human. For example, the Lord delivered you from your mother's womb. A child in the womb needs deliverance from so many things. You were susceptible to many dangers in the womb, the list is too numerous to mention. You could have being miscarried, aborted. You were born not by the power of your mother but by the benevolence and mercy of God. You did not come out a still born because of the Lord's mercies. No wonder when a woman gives birth, we say she has 'delivered', or the process of giving birth is referred to as 'child delivery'. We must never forget the most important person in the Delivery Process: that is, God, the Deliverer.

2 And he said, The LORD is my rock, and my fortress, and my deliverer; 3 The God of my rock; in him will I trust: he is my shield, and the horn of my salvation, my high tower, and my refuge, my saviour; thou savest me from violence. 4 I will call on the LORD, who is worthy to be praised: so shall I be saved from mine enemies. 5 When the waves of death compassed me, the floods of ungodly men made me afraid; 6 The sorrows of hell compassed me about; the snares of death prevented me; 7 In my distress I called upon the LORD, and cried to my God: and he did hear my voice out of his temple, and my cry did enter into his ears. 2 Sam 22:2-7 (KJV)

David remembered that there was a time he was in distress. He called upon the Lord in prayer and the Lord heard him. (2Sam.22:7). He believed that the same God will also hear him in his present trouble. He said he will therefore call on the Lord, who is worthy to be praised: and he shall be saved from his enemies.

7.   *Father, arise in Your power of old and show Yourself strong on my behalf in the name of Jesus.*

8.   *O Lord, You made a way in the red sea, arise and*

make a way for me where there seems to be no
way in the name of Jesus.

9. O God that answereth by fire, send Your revival
    fire to my city in my lifetime in the name of Jesus.

10. Father, I plug myself into Your covenant of mercy.
    Have mercy on me in the name of Jesus.

11. I prophesy that goodness and mercy shall follow
    me throughout this year and all the days of my life
    in Jesus' name.

12. Lord, let my life, business and profession attract
    grace and mercy from men and women of
    substance this year in the name of Jesus.

The Lord expressly commanded the children of Israel
to use this key of remembering His past merciful
deliverance whenever they were confronted by the
threats of their enemies. The strategic instruction is
found in *Deut.7:17-19.*

*17 If thou shalt say in thine heart, These nations
are more than I; how can I dispossess them?
18 Thou shalt not be afraid of them: but shalt
well remember what the LORD thy God did
unto Pharaoh, and unto all Egypt; 19 The great
temptations which thine eyes saw, and the signs,*

and the wonders, and the mighty hand, and the stretched out arm, whereby the LORD thy God brought thee out: so shall the LORD thy God do unto all the people of whom thou art afraid. Deut 7:17-19 (KJV)

We can see the practical application of this key in *Psalm 44:1-4*

1 We have heard with our ears, O God, our fathers have told us, what work thou didst in their days, in the times of old. 2 How thou didst drive out the heathen with thy hand, and plantedst them; how thou didst afflict the people, and cast them out. 3 For they got not the land in possession by their own sword, neither did their own arm save them: but thy right hand, and thine arm, and the light of thy countenance, because thou hadst a favour unto them. 4 Thou art my King, O God: command deliverances for Jacob. Psalms 44:1-4 (KJV)

Here, the psalmist acknowledged the past mercies of the Lord in delivering the people of God from their enemies and giving them victories. He recognized that it was not their power, strength or skill that gave them the land of their enemies but that God in His infinite mercy gave them favour. This realization must have given the Psalmist the courage and faith to pray the prayer he prayed in verse 4: "Thou art my King, O God, command deliverances for Jacob" or 'Decree victories for Jacob'.

You may be in some overwhelming situation right now. You are crushed on every side. Fear grips you and you are enveloped by doubts and uncertainties. You are been confronted by problems that are just too much for you to handle. All these are Pharaoh-like situations and the One who delivered Israel from Pharaoh is saying He will deliver you from the enemies that are too strong for you. Pharaoh boasted, yet he did not survive the red sea. Goliath boasted, yet he did not survive the stone of David. Herod boasted, yet he did not survive the sword of the angel and the consuming worms. In the same way, all the powers that are troubling your destiny will not survive the judgment of God in this season in Jesus' name. Only believe and trust in God.

13. *Father, by your great power and outstretched arm, deliver me from the contrary wind of life in the name of Jesus.*

14. *Every Goliath spirit tormenting my destiny,*

receive the stone of fire in the name of Jesus.

15. You stubborn Pharaoh spirit that will not let me go, I shall laugh last over you in the name of Jesus.

16. Herod spirit troubling the church, receive the anger and judgment of the Lord now in the name of Jesus.

17. The mountain before me, move by fire in the name of Jesus.

18. Lord, give me the grace to proclaim your word with boldness from now on in the name of Jesus.

19. The grace and mercy that make doors to open on their own accord, grant unto me this year in Jesus' name.

20. O Lord, remember me and in Your mercy, decree victories for me in the battles of life in the name of Jesus.

21. Lord, let me enter into abundance of Your grace and mercy this year in Jesus' name.

22. Thank You Almighty God, the same yesterday, today and forever more.

In troubled times, REMEMBER GOD'S PAST MERCIES. It is a winning key!

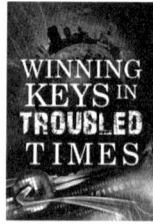

WINNING
KEYS IN
TROUBLED
TIMES

KEY THREE

REALIZE THAT IT IS COMMON

13 There hath no temptation taken you but such as is common to man: but God is faithful, who will not suffer you to be tempted above that ye are able; but will with the temptation also make a way to escape, that ye may be able to bear it. 1 Cor 10:13 (KJV)

When trials and troubles seem to overwhelm you and you are being tempted to want to give up and fall prey to satan, your adversary, you must realize that you are not the first to go through what you are going through. Many others have and survived. They held unto God in their trial. They refused to capitulate or compromise their faith and God did not disappoint them. He made a way of escape for them.

The enemy's greatest opportunity to tempt us to sin against God is during trials or troubled times. It was when Jesus Christ was hungry following a wilderness experience that satan came to tempt him. It was when Job had lost his possessions and children that satan came through his wife to tempt him to curse God and die. It was when Peter saw the Master being dragged to Golgotha in great pain and affliction that satan came to tempt him to deny Christ. In the face of a fiery furnace, the three Hebrew men were tempted to deny the living God and serve the idol of the heathen.

Whatever is your trouble today, it is common to man. Be it sickness, loss of job or a loved one, financial hardship, marital challenges, parental struggle, loneliness, business failure; academic setback; dashed hopes; unmet expectations; betrayal and disappointment. They are all common and you need not surrender to satan. God will surely make a way of escape for you.

19 Many are the afflictions of the righteous: but the LORD delivereth him out of them all. 20 He keepeth all his bones: not one of them is broken. Psalms 34:19-20 (KJV)

Your bones (strength, stability and stamina) may come under fiery assaults of the enemy but God says He will keep all your bones and not one of them will be broken. That means, no matter what, you will survive the storm. I know a sister who had an issue of blood and bled every day for seven months, but every time she remembered that God delivered another one who bled for twelve years, she received strength and hope that she will survive. She did survive and is alive and doing well as a wife and mother today. My own mother was diagnosed with cervical cancer and given a few months to live. It is now over four years since then and she is still alive, well and healthy. Glory to God.

Israel survived Pharaoh; The widow of Zeraphath survived famine; Hannah survived barrenness; King Hezekiah survived sickness and death sentence; Paul and Silas survived persecution; The Hebrew friends survived the fiery furnace; Daniel survived the Lion's den; Peter survived business failure; Mary Magdalene survived acute madness; Lazarus survived the power of the grave. Child of God, rejoice! You will survive!

1. *Father, command the fountain of my problem to dry up in the name of Jesus.*

2. *Every power behind prolonged affliction in my life, be paralysed in the name of Jesus.*

3. *Father, as You were the fourth man in the fire, be with me in all my trials in the name of Jesus.*

4. *I receive victory over the tempter in the mighty name of Jesus.*

5. *Every arrow of temptation fired at me, backfire now in the name of Jesus.*

6. *O Lord, no matter what, give me the grace never to deny You in the name of Jesus.*

7. *Every snare of death laid for me, catch your owners in the name of Jesus.*

8. *Father, don't let me do anything that I will later regret in the name of Jesus.*

9. *Holy Spirit, make me a flaming fire, too hot for the enemy of my soul to handle in the name of Jesus.*

10. *The grace to overcome every temptation to sin in the face of trials and troubles, come upon me mightily in the name of Jesus.*

33 These things I have spoken unto you, that in me ye might have peace. In the world ye shall have tribulation: but be of good cheer; I have overcome the world. John 16:33 (KJV)

Troubles and tribulations are common in this world, but be of good cheer. If Jesus overcame you too will overcome. Only surrender your life to Him completely. Do not yield to temptation and turn your back to God. Do not stop coming to church because of trials. Do not begin to seek ungodly solutions or some quick fix remedies that will end up compounding your situation. Rather put your trust in the One who says He will make a way.

Arthur W. Pink put it this way: *"Satan is ever seeking to inject that poison into our hearts to destrust God's goodness – especially in connection with his commandments. That is what really lies behind all evil, lusting and disobedience. A discontent with our position and portion, a craving from something which God has wisely held from us. Reject any suggestion that God is unduly severe with you. Resist with the utmost abhorrence anything that causes you to doubt God's love and his loving kindness toward you. Allow nothing to make you question the Father's love for his child".*

I love the way the Amplified version renders 1Cor.10:13:

> [13] *For no temptation (no trial regarded as enticing to sin), [no matter how it comes or where it leads] has overtaken you and laid hold on you that is not common to man [that is, no temptation or trial has come to you that is beyond human resistance and that is not adjusted and adapted and belonging to human experience, and such as man can bear]. But God is faithful [to His Word and to His compassionate nature], and He [can be trusted] not to let you be tempted and tried and assayed beyond your ability and strength of resistance and power to endure, but with the temptation He will [always] also provide the way out (the means of escape to a landing place), that you may be capable and strong and powerful to bear up under it patiently. 1 Cor 10:13 (AMP)*

It is written here that 'God is faithful'. Yes, He is faithful. Your health may not be faithful right now, but God is faithful. Your finances may not be faithful, but God is faithful. Your marriage may not be faithful, but God is faithful. Your children may not be faithful now, but God is faithful. Your career may not be faithful, but God is faithful.

'God is faithful' means: He is able. He is sufficient. He can do it. It is not impossible for Him to handle. It means He is a promise keeper. It means he will not delay nor deny. It means He will turn your ashes to beauty. It means He will not allow your expectations to be cut short. He is faithful and would not allow you to be afflicted, denied, persecuted, mocked, and messed up, rubbished, beaten, battered or bruised beyond what you are able to bear. He is faithful to make a way for you to overcome it all.

If he made a way in the red sea, there is a way for you in that situation right now. There are many things He can do to open that gate militating against your breakthrough. He can command it to lift up its head. Ps.24:7-10. He can send an angel to open the gate because the Key of David is in His hands. He can also command the gate to open of its own accord. Acts 12:10.

11. *Every barrier blocking my way of escape, I bulldoze you now in the name of Jesus.*

12. *Gates saying no to my breakthrough, you are a liar, lift up your head now in the name of Jesus.*

13. *Every power cutting short my expectations, I cut you off now in the name of Jesus.*

14. *O Lord, arise, manifest your power in my situation in the name of Jesus.*

15. *Gates of brass challenging my victory, be broken down in the name of Jesus.*

16. *Bars of iron assigned against my destiny, be cut into pieces in the name of Jesus.*

17. *Angel of my breakthrough, appear now in my favour in the name of Jesus.*

18. *Power to travail in prayer until I prevail, come upon me now in the name of Jesus.*

19. *Holy Spirit, help me to be sensitive to your promptings in the name of Jesus.*

20. *My ears, be opened to receive divine directions and instructions in the name of Jesus.*

21. *Father, open the eyes of my understanding and let me see great and mighty things; let me behold your wondrous works in the name of Jesus.*

In troubled times, REALIZE THAT IT IS COMMON and refuse to yield to temptations to sin. It is a winning key!

KEY FOUR

RENEW YOUR STRENGTH

17 Although the fig tree shall not blossom, neither shall fruit be in the vines; the labour of the olive shall fail, and the fields shall yield no meat; the flock shall be cut off from the fold, and there shall be no herd in the stalls: 18 Yet I will rejoice in the LORD, I will joy in the God of my salvation. 19 The LORD God is my strength, and he will make my feet like hinds' feet, and he will make me to walk upon mine high places. Hab 3:17-19 (KJV)

P rophet Habbakuk declared that in spite of the troubled times facing him, he will rejoice in the Lord because the Lord is His strength. He will draw strength from the Lord and very soon, all his troubles would become his footstool.

The bible says: *¹⁰ If you falter in times of trouble, how small is your strength! Prov 24:10 (NIV)*. This means that in troubled times, you cannot afford to lack strength or be weak, small or insufficient in strength for that matter.

When Nehemiah and his people were troubled by their adversaries on every side, he encouraged them powerfully by saying to them:

And be not grieved and depressed, for the joy of the Lord is your strength and stronghold. Neh 8:10 (AMP)

1. *Father, I thank You for the spirit of love, power and sound mind that You have given me.*
2. *Every arrow of sorrow and depression being fired at me, return to your sender in the name of Jesus.*
3. *O Lord, deliver me from shedding tears of sorrow in the name of Jesus.*
4. *I hereby receive beauty for ashes and garment of*

praise in exchange for mourning in the name of Jesus.

5.   *I confess: The joy of the Lord is my strength and stronghold in the name of Jesus.*

6.   *Father, send me helpers of joy in the name of Jesus.*

7.   *I refuse to be a victim of miserable comforters in the mighty name of Jesus.*

There is a wonderful passage in the bible about the need to renew your strength in troubled times:

27 Why sayest thou, O Jacob, and speakest, O Israel, My way is hid from the LORD, and my judgment is passed over from my God? 28 Hast thou not known? hast thou not heard, that the everlasting God, the LORD, the Creator of the ends of the earth, fainteth not, neither is weary? there is no searching of his understanding. 29 He giveth power to the faint; and to them that have no might he increaseth strength. 30 Even the youths shall faint and be weary, and the young men shall utterly fall: 31 But they that wait upon the LORD shall renew their strength; they shall mount up with wings as eagles; they shall run, and not be weary; and they shall walk, and not faint. Isaiah 40:27-31 (KJV)

In the above story, which I believe many of us can relate to, Jacob was complaining to God. He lamented that God did not see his troubles. God ignored his rights, he said. He felt despised, rejected and discarded by God. The Lord then reminded Jacob that unlike him, he, God, never grows weary or weak. God made it clear Jacob's complaints were symptoms of spiritual weakness and he needed to seek God for strength. The Lord declared that mortal men will grow weak and weary but it is God that will never faint nor lose strength. He is the Omnipotent One. He invited Jacob to come and exchange his weakness for God's strength instead of lamenting in his troubled times.

When circumstances seem to overwhelm us and we are losing our strength, the solution is to wait on the Lord for a spiritual recharge and renewal of strength.

14 Wait on the LORD: be of good courage, and he shall strengthen thine heart: wait, I say, on the LORD. Psalms 27:13-14 (KJV)

34 Wait on the LORD, and keep his way, and he shall exalt thee to inherit the land: when the wicked are cut off, thou shalt see it. 35 I have seen the wicked in great power, and spreading himself like a green bay tree. 36 Yet he passed away, and, lo, he was not: yea, I sought him, but he could not be found. Psalms 37:34-36 (KJV)

In effect, if you wait on the Lord, you will laugh last. That wickedness will pass away; that storm will soon calm down; that evil cloud will shortly be rolled away. That trouble has not come to stay put, very soon you will be saying: "yet, it passed away, and lo, it was not...".

Hannah Witall Smith said: "The soul that waits upon the Lord is the soul that is entirely surrendered to Him and that trusts Him perfectly. Therefore we might name our wings the wings of Surrender and of Trust. If we will only surrender ourselves utterly to the Lord, and will trust Him perfectly, we shall find our souls "mounting up with wings as eagles" to the "heavenly places" in Christ Jesus, where earthly annoyances or sorrows have no power to disturb us."

PRACTICAL STEPS TO WAIT ON THE LORD

- Dedicate time alone with God. Jacob wrestled with God in Gen.32:26 and said *"I will not let thee go, except thou bless me"*.
- Give God quality praise, worship and thanksgiving for His kindness; goodness and mercy.
- Study and meditate on the Scriptures particularly God's promises for your situation. Confess such promises aloud as they apply to your case.
- Confess and repent from any known sin or every issue that comes under the convicting power of the Holy Spirit as you wait on the Lord.
- Listen to sound teachings and preaching of the word of God. Release your heart to receive the truth and be willing to abide by God's word.
- Cast out all fears, worries and anxiety. Phil.4:6-8.
- Subdue your flesh and elevate your spirit by fasting as you are led by the Spirit.
- Pray aggressively concerning the situation and never quit praying until you break through. Lk.18:1 enjoins us to pray always and not to quit.
- Find a trusted prayer partner to agree with in prayer because one will chase a thousand and two will put ten thousand to flight. Dt.32:30. Moreover Jesus Christ promised answer when two or three of you

agree in prayer on a particular matter.Matt.18:19.

- Be an Eagle Christian. To mount up with fresh wings of strength and power, the eagle often hibernates for a period of time, shed off the old feathers and grow new one. If you and I also want power to confront and conquer the vicissitudes of our times, we must hibernate in the secret place of the Most High in order to rejuvenate with soaring ability.

- Like the Eagle, which is able to look straight at the sun, you must fix your gaze at the Sun of Righteousness. Mal.4:2. You must look unto Jesus, the author and finisher of our faith. Heb.12:2. Cast your burden unto the Lord, for he cares for you.

- The Eagle is a secret place animal. She builds her nest in the most inaccessible place on top of the rock. You too must wait on the Lord by retreating into the secret place of the Most High that you may abide in the shadow of the Almighty. The secret place of prayer is the solution place for problems. Ps.91:1-2.

25 The LORD is good unto them that wait for him, to the soul that seeketh him. 26 It is good that a man should both hope and quietly wait for the salvation of the LORD. Lam 3:24-26 (KJV)

Pray the following prayers now:

8. *Father, I praise You, the All- Mighty and All-Powerful God.*

9. *Thank You Father for being my Strength, my Shield, my Buckler and the Rock of my Salvation.*

10. *Father, forgive me for every sin of murmuring and complaining I have committed against You in Jesus name.*

11. *Father, forgive me for my sin of prayerlessness and general spiritual carelessness in the name of Jesus.*

12. *Every mark of frustration and discouragement in my life, be wiped off by the blood of Jesus.*

13. *My Father, lead me to the Rock that is higher than I in the name of Jesus.*

14. *Eagle anointing to fly above my mountains, come upon me mightily in the name of Jesus.*

15. *Power for exceeding and abundant exploits in life, come upon me in the name of Jesus.*

16. *Father, you renewed the strength of Elijah for the journey, renew my strength too in the name of Jesus.*

17. *O Lord arise and avenge me of my adversaries in the name of Jesus.*

18. *Father, give me strength to bring forth my long*

awaited miracle this year in the name of Jesus.

19. *Arrows of discouragement fired at me, you shall not prosper in the name of Jesus.*

20. *Robbers of my time alone with God, scatter in the name of Jesus.*

21. *Father, send forth the Rod of Strength on my behalf and give me dominion in the midst of my enemies in the name of Jesus.*

22. *Father, give me holy detention in Your presence and let my joy be full in the name of Jesus.*

23. *By faith, I receive power to mount up with wings and I soar above my present limitations in the name of Jesus.*

24. *Every virtue, strength and glory stolen by the enemy of my soul, be restored sevenfold in the name of Jesus.*

25. *Let my youth be renewed like the Eagle's in the name of Jesus.*

26. *I come against the spirit of heaviness, come out of my life now in the name of Jesus.*

27. *Lord make me a prayer eagle in the mighty name of Jesus.*

28. *The strength to travail and prevail in prayer, come upon me mightily in Jesus' name.*

29. *The eagle lives for long, in the name of Jesus, I*

will be satisfied with long life.

30. *Every demon empowering sin in my life, be roasted by fire in the name of Jesus.*

31. *Father, give me a divine exchange in your presence in the name of Jesus.*

32. *Thou Sun of Righteousness, touch me with Your healing wings in the name of Jesus.*

33. *Powers assigned to hunt down my destiny, turn back by fire in the name of Jesus.*

34. *I fire back every arrow of frustration and discouragement in the place of prayer in the name of Jesus.*

35. *O Lord, exalt my horn and anoint me with fresh oil in the name of Jesus.*

36. *Thank You Lord because my waiting on You shall never be in vain.*

When you find yourself in troubled times, RENEW YOUR STRENGTH. It is a Winning key.

KEY FIVE

RELEASE YOUR FAITH

17 Although the fig tree shall not blossom, neither shall fruit be in the vines; the labour of the olive shall fail, and the fields shall yield no meat; the flock shall be cut off from the fold, and there shall be no herd in the stalls: 18 Yet I will rejoice in the LORD, I will joy in the God of my salvation. 19 The LORD God is my strength, and he will make my feet like hinds' feet, and he will make me to walk upon mine high places. Hab 3:17-19 (KJV)

The prophet said in spite of the adverse situation and circumstances confronting him, he will rejoice and joy in the God of his salvation. He maintained his confidence, belief and trust in God that he will soon be riding over his adversaries. That is the kind of faith that can launch a man into the realm of the supernatural. When you speak like that to the kingdom of darkness, they tremble and scatter.

Listen to David:

> *8 It is better to trust in the LORD than to put confidence in man. 9 It is better to trust in the LORD than to put confidence in princes. 10 All nations compassed me about: but in the name of the LORD will I destroy them. 11 They compassed me about; yea, they compassed me about: but in the name of the LORD I will destroy them. 12 They compassed me about like bees; they are quenched as the fire of thorns: for in the name of the LORD I will destroy them Psalms 118:8-12 (KJV)*

David released his faith to confront his overwhelming situation. He did not keep quiet, accept defeat or give up in the face of stronger adversaries. Instead, he confessed his faith in God to help him destroy the enemies. God loves those who have faith in Him.

6 But without faith it is impossible to please him: for he that cometh to God must believe that he is, and that he is a rewarder of them that diligently seek him. Heb 11:6 (KJV)

1. *Father, deliver me from every spirit of doubt limiting me from pleasing You.*
2. *O Lord, increase my faith in the name of Jesus.*
3. *You spirit of fear troubling my mind, melt away by fire in the name of Jesus.*
4. *Lord, make me a man after Your own heart who will fulfil all your will in the mighty name of Jesus.*
5. *Powers surrounding me like bees, I destroy you in the name of the Lord Jesus Christ.*
6. *Every fiery dart of the enemy aimed at paralysing my faith, be dashed to pieces in the name of Jesus.*
7. *Lord, I lift up my eyes unto You for my help comes from You in Jesus name.*
8. *O Lord, You are my present help in times of need, arise and help my unbelief in the name of Jesus.*

Troubled times are like giant obstacles confronting us. They can be daunting and overwhelming. If you are working hard with little to show for it, there is a problem. Many have their homes under threats of repossession because of these troubled times. Some who used to have well paid jobs do not have anything at all right now. Some do not even know what more prayers to pray for their miracles to manifest. Everywhere some of us turn, there is a roadblock. That roadblock, obstacle, barrier, trouble or hindrance is a 'Goliath'. The strategy David used to defeat his Goliath was to release words of faith against this stubborn pursuer. It worked! It will work for you too in Jesus name.

45 Then said David to the Philistine, Thou comest to me with a sword, and with a spear, and with a shield: but I come to thee in the name of the LORD of hosts, the God of the armies of Israel, whom thou hast defied. 46 This day will the LORD deliver thee into mine hand; and I will smite thee, and take thine head from thee; and I will give the carcases of the host of the Philistines this day unto the fowls of the air, and to the wild beasts of the earth; that all the earth may know that there is a God in Israel. 47 And all this assembly shall know that the LORD saveth not with sword and spear: for the battle is the LORD'S, and he will *give you into our hands. **48** And it came to pass, when the Philistine arose, and came and drew nigh to meet David, that David hasted, and ran toward the army to meet the Philistine. **49** And David put his hand in his bag, and took thence a stone, and slang it, and smote the Philistine in his forehead, that the stone sunk into his forehead; and he fell upon his face to the earth. **50** So David prevailed over the Philistine with a sling and with a stone, and smote the Philistine, and slew him; but there was no sword in the hand of David. **51** Therefore David ran, and stood upon the Philistine, and took his sword, and drew it out of the sheath thereof, and slew him, and cut off his head therewith. And when the Philistines saw their champion was dead, they fled. 1 Sam 17:45-51 (KJV)*

David had already painted the picture of the fallen Goliath while the latter was still standing tall. David sent out invitation cards to the fowls of the air and the wild beasts of the earth to come and eat 'Goliath head pepper soup'. David called those things that be not as though they were already. He was releasing his faith.

Jesus, our Lord said:

22 And Jesus answering saith unto them, Have faith in God. 23 For verily I say unto you, That whosoever shall say unto this mountain, Be thou removed, and be thou cast into the sea; and shall not doubt in his heart, but shall believe that those things which he saith shall come to pass; he shall have whatsoever he saith. 24 Therefore I say unto you, What things soever ye desire, when ye pray, believe that ye receive them, and ye shall have them.
Mark 11:22-24 (KJV)

Pray now:
9.   *Goliath assigned against my destiny, right now, be wasted in the name of Jesus.*
10. *Every verdict of darkness concerning my wellbeing, be reversed now in Jesus' name.*
11. *Giant obstacles to my promotion, be rolled back in the name of Jesus.*
12. *Evil tongues, speaking divination and enchantments against my star, be rendered dumb in the name of Jesus.*
13. *Mountains of adversity, be removed now in the name of Jesus.*

14. *Any power hiding the key of my promotion, be paralysed in the name of Jesus.*

15. *Father, You are the Man of war, arise and fight my battles for me in the name of Jesus.*

16. *You gathering storms against my fruitfulness, scatter in the name of Jesus.*

17. *Every sickness assigned to kill me, hear the word of the Lord, you are not unto death in the name of Jesus.*

18. *All boasting Goliaths delegated against my next level, you shall not prosper in the name of Jesus.*

19. *Father, reverse all curses operating against my family and turn them to blessings in the name of Jesus.*

20. *Every hindrance to my greatness, begin to give way right now in the name of Jesus.*

Faith is the currency of heaven. If you spend it, you will have plenty of divine goods. Faith is calling those things that are not as though they were. Heb.11:1 says *"Now faith is the substance of things hoped for, the evidence of things not seen"*. It is the unwavering and unflinching belief and trust in God. Where there is faith, there is no fear and no doubt. Faith is described as acting out your expectations without considering your limitations. 99% of those who came to Jesus for healing heard him say: "Thy faith had made thee whole" and they were indeed healed. *Matt.9:22; 15:28; Mark 10:52; Luke 17:19.*

A woman was diagnosed with a terminal disease; she went to a prayer mountain at the counsel of her pastor. She spent seven days in prayer and fasting and her only prayer point was to release words of faith into her situation by declaring thus: "Thank You Jesus, I am healed by Your stripes". She said this declaratory prayer over and over for more than ten thousand times. She came down from that prayer mountain completely whole. Her faith made her whole. Some other people in her position would have died of fear ten times before their death. While Saul and others were full of fear at the sight of Goliath, David was full of faith. Steve Maraboli said: *"Your fear is 100% dependent on you for its survival".* Pray like this: "I hereby divorce myself from every spirit of fear in the name of Jesus"

Mother Teresa said: *"God will never, never, never let us down if we have faith and put our trust in Him. He will always look after us. So we must cleave to Jesus. Our whole life must simply be woven into Jesus".*

Wherever faith is, favour always shows up. By faith, Abraham obeyed God and was willing to offer Isaac; the favour of eternal blessing was his reward. By faith Esther approached the king uninvited and contrary to the law and custom of the land, she obtained favour and her desires were granted. By faith Nehemiah prayed and took steps to make a near impossible request from the king, he obtained favour and the king granted him more than he needed. Ruth approached Boaz's field by faith, she obtained favour as her reward. By faith, the woman with the issue of blood touched Jesus' garment; favour located and healed her. By faith Blind Bartmeaus cried to Jesus when forces around him tried to silence him; he obtained his miracle as grace and mercy stood still in his favour.

Those who continue to live in sin, in disobedience to God and in unbridled prayerlessness cannot claim to have faith. They are not pleasing God. They cannot survive troubled times, though it comes upon them.

17 The righteous cry, and the LORD heareth, and delivereth them out of all their troubles. 18 The LORD is nigh unto them that are of a broken heart; and saveth such as be of a *contrite spirit. **19** Many are the afflictions of the righteous: but the LORD delivereth him out of them all. **20** He keepeth all his bones: not one of them is broken. Psalms 34:17-20 (KJV)*

That scripture makes it clear that it is the cry of the righteous that the Lord listens to. It also affirms that though the afflictions or troubles of the righteous may be many, but the Lord will deliver him out of them all. Your bones may be bruised, but it will not be broken. Every good thing the enemy has cut off in your destiny shall be restored this year in Jesus name.

***7** For there is hope of a tree, if it be cut down, that it will sprout again, and that the tender branch thereof will not cease. **8** Though the root thereof wax old in the earth, and the stock thereof die in the ground; **9** Yet through the scent of water it will bud, and bring forth boughs like a plant. Job 14:7-9 (KJV)*

I speak the word of faith into your life and prophesy that your haggard health will sprout again; your failing finances will sprout again; your cascading career will sprout again; your manacled marriage will sprout again and your fuzzy future will sprout again in the name of Jesus Christ.

To win in troubled times, right your relationship with God and then release your faith to challenge the mountain. Pray the following prayers aloud now:

21. *I confess that Greater is He that is in me than he that is in the world; therefore, I shall not be put to shame in the name of Jesus.*

22. *No evil shall befall my family and no plague shall come near us in the name of Jesus.*

23. *O Lord that stills the storm, still every storm raging around me in Jesus' name.*

24. *Spirit of failure at the edge of success, I am not your candidate; depart from me now in the name of Jesus.*

25. *O Lord, I receive the grace to live in total obedience to God. Therefore I shall eat the good of the land in the name of Jesus.*

26. *Adversaries of my open doors, scatter by fire in the name of Jesus.*

27. *Every power saying to me 'Come down', let fire fall from heaven and consume you in Jesus' name.*

28. *Every conquered enemy seeking reinforcement against me, you are a liar; be silenced forever in*

the name of Jesus.

29. *Father, let my joy be full and do not permit the enemy to pollute my testimony in the name of Jesus.*

30. *Every power assigned to turn my jubilation to humiliation, die by fire in the name of Jesus.*

31. *I hereby receive jubilee miracles for all those who have come to celebrate the faithfulness of God with me in the name of Jesus.*

32. *When Pharaoh was buried alive, he never rose again, let every stubborn power assigned against my progress be buried alive in the name of Jesus.*

33. *O Lord, the Prince of peace, decree peace to every troublesome situation in my life in the name of Jesus.*

34. *Jubilee blessings, favour, promotion and restoration, locate me and all my loved ones this year in the name of Jesus.*

35. *Let every satanic plan to embarrass me this year be dissolved in the name of Jesus.*

36. *Every council of hell summoned to truncate my testimony, scatter by fire in the name of Jesus.*

37. *Every leakage of my virtue, be sealed by the blood of Jesus.*

38. *Father, where men say there is no way for me to*

breakthrough, make a way for me there in the name of Jesus.

39. *As the Lord lives, I shall live my days in pleasure not pressure and my years in prosperity, not poverty in the name of Jesus.*

40. *I thank You Father for making my feet strong like hind's feet and for giving me wings to soar above the mountains in the name of Jesus.*

When troubled times stare you in the face, RELEASE YOUR FAITH. It is a winning key!

KEY SIX

RECOVER ALL

*17 Even though the fig trees are all destroyed,
and there is neither blossom left nor fruit;
though the olive crops all fail, and the fields lie
barren; even if the flocks die in the fields and
the cattle barns are empty, 18 yet I will rejoice
in the Lord; I will be happy in the God of my
salvation. 19 The Lord God is my strength; he
will give me the speed of a deer and bring me
safely over the mountains. Hab 3:17-19 (TLB)*

I would like you to note verse 19 of the above
scripture. In troubled times, the prophet declared
thus: *"The Lord is my strength; he will give me the
speed of a deer and bring me safely over the
mountains"*. What that simply tells us is that though

the times are hard and full of trouble, yet there is hope of total recovery. The man was wise enough not to give up. He saw victory in sight. He saw himself reaching the top of the mountain and overcoming the obstacles. He was determined to recover all. That is a major key to hold unto in troubled times. No retreat, no surrender to the situation, no matter how challenging it may be. Quitters never win and winners never quit.

4 And the ark rested in the seventh month, on the seventeenth day of the month, upon the mountains of Ararat. 5 And the waters decreased continually until the tenth month: in the tenth month, on the first day of the month, were the tops of the mountains seen. Gen 8:4-5 (KJV)

I prophesy that the ark of your destiny will find perfect rest. The waters of affliction against you will not increase. Rather it will decrease continually from now until you shall see it completely dried up. This year, you shall see the top of that mountain in the mighty name of Jesus.

Pray like this:

1. *My ladder of total recovery, appear to me now in the name of Jesus.*

2. *O hand of the Lord, come upon me and give me divine acceleration in the name of Jesus.*

3. *Every hopeless situation confronting my destiny, your time is up, turn around now in the name of Jesus.*

4. *Ascending and descending angels of my glory, show up now in the name of Jesus.*

5. *Father, take me to Bethel and covenant me for greatness in the mighty name of Jesus.*

6. *Powers that have vowed to put permanent roadblocks on my way to the top, be paralysed now in the name of Jesus.*

7. *Thou destroying mountains, you will be destroyed in the name of Jesus.*

8. *This year, I shall see the top of this mountain in the mighty name of Jesus. (Mention the mountains confronting you and prophetically declare yourself on top of them all)*

Whatever you lost during the raging wind of troubled times is subject to recovery or restoration. *In Jer.30:17, God said: "For I will restore health unto thee and I will heal thee of thy wounds... ".* You must always tune your mind to the great possibility of coming out of that storm stronger and better than when you went into it.

> *10 And the LORD turned the captivity of Job, when he prayed for his friends: also the LORD gave Job twice as much as he had before. Job 42:10 (KJV)*

The troubles of Job seemed like eternity, but in truth it never lasted, but Job lasted! *16 After this lived Job an hundred and forty years, and saw his sons, and his sons' sons, even four generations. Job 42:16 (KJV).* I prophesy to you the reader that 'after this (trouble you are in right now)' your brand new beginning of joy unspeakable will be unleashed in Jesus' name. Gregory Peck said: *"Tough times don't last, tough people do, remember?"*

9.   *Father, command restoration of all that the enemy had stolen from me in the name of Jesus.*
10. *All my goods in satanic warehouse, what are you still doing there, come out and return to me now in the name of Jesus.*
11. *Father, let my failure disappear and let my*

breakthrough appear in the name of Jesus.

12. *Father, let my barrenness disappear and let my fruitfulness appear in Jesus name.*

13. *Father, let my shame disappear and let my fame appear in the name of Jesus.*

14. *Father, let my pains disappear and let my gains appear in the name of Jesus.*

15. *Father, let divine message appear out of my mess in the name of Jesus.*

16. *Father, let my labour disappear and let my favour appear in the name of Jesus.*

17. *Father, let my disgrace disappear and let Your amazing grace appear in the name of Jesus.*

18. *O Lord, uproot evil things from my life and plant good things into my life in Jesus name.*

19. *Stubborn yokes of the enemy in my life, be destroyed in the name of Jesus.*

20. *Wicked hindrances to my greatness, begin to give way now in Jesus' name.*

21. *Arrows of oppression, backfire and return to sender in the name of Jesus.*

22. *I renounce every agreement with defeat and death in the name of Jesus.*

23. *Robbers of my joy, receive fire now in the name of Jesus.*

24. *Father, restore virtue unto me sevenfold in the name of Jesus.*
25. *Ancestral thieves and robbers, return the glory you stole from my family in the name of Jesus.*
26. *Altars of affliction, your time is up, catch fire and burn to ashes in the name of Jesus.*

DAVID RECOVERED ALL, YOU TOO MUST...

1 And it came to pass, when David and his men were come to Ziklag on the third day, that the Amalekites had invaded the south, and Ziklag, and smitten Ziklag, and burned it with fire; 2 And had taken the women captives, that were therein: they slew not any, either great or small, but carried them away, and went on their way. 3 So David and his men came to the city, and, behold, it was burned with fire; and their wives, and their sons, and their daughters, were taken captives. 4 Then David and the people that were with him lifted up their voice and wept, until they had no more power to weep. 5 And David's two wives were taken captives, Ahinoam the Jezreelitess, and Abigail the wife of Nabal the Carmelite. 6 And David was greatly distressed; for the people spake of stoning him, because the soul of all the people was grieved, every man for his sons and for his daughters: but David encouraged himself in the LORD his God. 7 And David said to Abiathar the priest, Ahimelech's son, I pray thee, bring me hither the ephod. And Abiathar brought thither the ephod to David. 8 And David enquired at the LORD, saying, Shall I pursue after this troop? shall I overtake them? And he answered him, Pursue: for thou shalt surely overtake them, and without fail recover all. 1 Sam 30:1-8 (KJV)

18 And David recovered all that the Amalekites had carried away: and David rescued his two wives. 19 And there was nothing lacking to them, neither small nor great, neither sons nor daughters, neither spoil, nor any thing that they had taken to them: David recovered all. 1 Sam 30:18-19 (KJV)

David experienced troubled times. He went to battle with his army. By the time he returned to his camp in Ziglag, the Amalekites, arch enemies of Israel had invaded Ziglag, burnt it down and held captives his wives, children and also the families of his soldiers. Everybody was so sad and angry that they planned to stone David for not protecting them against the band of raiders. David too wept until he lost the strength to weep. When he saw that weeping will not solve the problem, he went to God in prayer and God told him to rise up, pursue the enemies, overtake them and surely recover all they have stolen from him and his soldiers. God is never on the side of weepers over problem, He is on the side of seekers of solution to problems.

15 And the LORD said unto Moses, Wherefore criest thou unto me? speak unto the children of Israel, that they go forward: Ex 14:15 (KJV)

Edwin Louis Cole said: *"You don't drown by falling in the water, you drown by staying there"* Your health, wealth, career, marriage, freedom, anointing or opportunities might have falling in the water. They are not drowned until you allow them to stay there. You can get up and pick them up again. Remember *"...the violent taketh it by force". Matt.11:12.*

HOW TO RECOVER ALL

ONE: You must stop weeping, mourning, moaning, complaining or blaming anyone for your situation. Do not surrender your joy to the enemy. The joy of the Lord is your strength. Weeping will make you lose your vision when your face is covered with tears of sorrow and when you lose your vision, you lose direction to recovery. *Job 17:7 "Mine eye also is dim by reason of sorrow and all my members are as a shadow".*

27. *I terminate the night of weeping from my destiny; I declare my new dawn of joy in the name of Jesus.*

28. *Let tears of sorrow be far away from me O Lord, only tears of joy shall fill my eyes in the name of Jesus.*

29. *Father, send me helpers of joy from the four corners of the earth in the name of Jesus.*

30. *I confess, the joy of the Lord is my strength in Jesus' name.*

31. *Every sorrow of heart assigned to break my spirit, I am not your candidate, be far from me in the name of Jesus.*

32. *I receive deliverance from the oppression of the devil by the blood of Jesus.*

33. *Father, let no one have cause to say to me: "this is nothing else but sorrow of heart" in the name of Jesus.*

34. *Father, while my adversaries cry for sorrow of heart, let me sing for joy of heart according to your word in Isa.65:14 in the name of Jesus.*

35. *O Lord, turn all my mourning to dancing; ashes to beauty and change my garment of pain to that of praise in the name of Jesus.*

36. *This year, with joy, I shall draw water from the well of salvation in the name of Jesus.*

TWO: Encourage Yourself in the Lord: *6 And David was greatly distressed; for the people spake of stoning him, because the soul of all the people was grieved, every man for his sons and for his daughters: but David encouraged himself in the LORD his God. 1 Sam 30:6 (KJV).*

You must discourage your discouragement during troubled times. Many, as a result of discouragement have become frustrated and fallen into depression. Some have committed suicide, taken wrong course in life and had their destinies truncated due to discouragement. In 1Kings 17, when famine (economic recession) hit the city, a widow almost committed suicide with her only son. The Psalmist said: *"Why am I discouraged? Why is my heart so sad? I will put my hope in God! I will praise him again, my Saviour and my God!" Ps.42:11.* When discouragement seems to set in, learn to speak encouraging words to yourself or to the victim of discouragement.

10 Say ye to the righteous, that it shall be well with him: for they shall eat the fruit of their doings. Isaiah 3:10 (KJV)

There was a time my wife became so discouraged as a result of the adverse troubles confronting us, she said in frustration: "When will all these problems end". I raised my voice to encourage her and discourage discouragement by saying: "It will end this year". Sure enough, the mountain became level ground that same year. I prophesy to the reader of this book, your mountain shall become level ground this year in Jesus name.

"It is said an Eastern monarch once charged his wise men to invent him a sentence to be ever in view, and which should be true and appropriate in all times and

situations. They presented him the words: "And this, too, shall pass away." Abraham Lincoln.

37. *Every contrary wind raging against my destiny, you have not come to stay, you have come to pass away in the name of Jesus.*
38. *Storm or no storm, I will reach my destiny destination in the name of Jesus.*
39. *Every plant of discouragement in my life, be uprooted now in Jesus name.*
40. *Every demonic marriage orchestrated for my life, be dissolved now in the name of Jesus.*
41. *Tragedy, I am not your candidate; you shall not locate me in the name of Jesus.*
42. *Every warring power against my destiny dream, scatter now in Jesus name.*
43. *Pharaoh that wants me to die in captivity, the red sea is waiting to swallow you up in the name of Jesus.*
44. *I discourage my discouragement and frustrate my frustration. Let me go in the name of Jesus.*

THREE: Take it to the Lord in Prayer. *7 And David said to Abiathar the priest, Ahimelech's son, I pray thee, bring me hither the ephod. And*

*Abiathar brought thither the ephod to David.
8 And David enquired at the LORD, saying,
Shall I pursue after this troop? shall I
overtake them? And he answered him,
Pursue: for thou shalt surely overtake them,
and without fail recover all. 1 Sam 30:7-8
(KJV)*

The place of prayer is the place of enquiry for direction
in times of confusion. It is the place of comfort in times
of concern. It is the place of power and strength in
times of weakness. When the storms of troubled times
seem so fierce against us, we must learn to cry to God
in prayer. Prayer works. Prayer is eternal. Prayer does
not die. God hears and answers prayer. *2 O thou that
hearest prayer, unto thee shall all flesh come Psalms
65:1-2 (KJV).* In the race of life, prayerful preparation
prevents poor performance. God said in *Jer.33:3*
*"3 Call unto me, and I will answer thee, and
shew thee great and mighty things, which thou
knowest not".*

David did not receive the key to recover all in the place
of weeping; rather, he received it in the place of prayer.
Go and do likewise in your present situation.

45. *Fresh fire from heaven, fall upon my prayer life in the name of Jesus.*

46. *Father, order my steps and lead me in the way that I should go in the name of Jesus.*

47. *O Lord, open my eyes to see divine prescriptions to my problems in the name of Jesus.*

48. *Troublers of my Israel, your time is up, this day, you shall be troubled in the name of Jesus.*

49. *I bind every spirit of heaviness in me in the name of Jesus.*

50. *Every operation of wasters in my life is hereby terminated for good in the name of Jesus.*

51. *The rope of affliction tying me down, catch fire and be burnt to ashes in the name of Jesus.*

52. *Thou spirit of prayer, come upon me mightily in the name of Jesus.*

53. *My prayer life will not be sacrificed on the altar of discouragement and frustration in the name of Jesus.*

54. *Power to pray when I don't feel like praying; pray when I feel like praying and pray until I feel like praying, fall upon me now in the name of Jesus.*

55. *Delilah spirit assigned against my anointing, die by fire in the name of Jesus.*

56. *Jezebel spirit assigned to steal and destroy my*

inheritance, die by fire in the name of Jesus.
57. Ahab's spirit of oppression and depression,
evaporate from my life in Jesus' name.

FOUR: Arise and Pursue. *10 But David pursued, he and four hundred men: 1 Sam 30:10 (KJV).* The essence of the key of recovering all is that after you have sought the face of God in prayer, you must be prepared to move. Aggressive pursuers are progressive people.

You must be a doer of the word according to James 1:22. To recover your financial destiny, you must give bountifully as God says in 2Cor.9:6; to recover your portion of the good of the land, you must be willing and obedient according to Isa.1:19. To recover all the devourer had stolen from your destiny, you must begin to give your tithe and not rob God of it. Mal.3:10. To have all your prayers answered, you must be winning souls according to John 15:16. To recover your business, practice diligence. If you have been diligent before, become more diligent. Hard work does not kill the hard worker, rather, hard work does kiss the hard worker with robust rewards.

God did not promise a smooth sail, free ride in the journey of life. Jesus said in this world you will have tribulations. What God guaranteed is our triumph as long as we stand with him. In effect, the enemy has no power over you except the one you yield to him. He is out to contend with you at every level. For every next level you attain in life, there is a next devil waiting to confront you, but when you return fire for fire, he will leave you alone.

A brother went to lament to his pastor that some forces were shooting him in his dream and every night it was getting worse. He did not know what to do anymore. The pastor said whenever they shoot him in the dream, he too should wake up and prophetically shoot back. He obeyed and practiced this. It worked and the devil left him alone. Someone said : *"A bend in the road is not the end of the road...unless you fail to make the turn"*. Arise and make that turn for it is your long awaited turn around!

58. *Every stubborn pursuer assigned against me, turn back by fire in the name of Jesus.*

59. *Amalekites powers that have stolen my inheritance, you will vomit it this year in the name of Jesus.*

60. *You devourer, my health is not your property, vomit it now in the name of Jesus.*
61. *Father, anoint me to press on to the mark of the prize of the high calling of Christ Jesus.*
62. *I refuse to remain on the ground, I move forward by fire this year in Jesus' name.*
63. *As I pursue God, every good thing, begin to pursue me in the name of Jesus.*

FIVE: WITHOUT FAIL, RECOVER ALL. *18 And David recovered all that the Amalekites had carried away: and David rescued his two wives. 19 And there was nothing lacking to them, neither small nor great, neither sons nor daughters, neither spoil, nor any thing that they had taken to them: David recovered all. 20 And David took all the flocks and the herds, which they drave before those other cattle, and said, This is David's spoil. 1 Sam 30:18-20 (KJV)*

The wonder of this key is that you will recover much more than the troubled times stole from you. When Job recovered, he had more than he lost to the troubled times. When David recovered all, he recovered not only what the Amalekites stole from him but what they stole from other cities as well. He had more than enough to keep and to share. Never limit God. He is able to do more than you can ever ask or think of. Eph.3:20.

Before the storm, David probably had just enough for himself, his army and their families. But after surviving the storm, he had so much that he distributed spoils of war to 13 CITIES. There is divine purpose in demonic problem. I prophesy that you will not borrow but lend unto nations in the name of Jesus. Col. Harland Sanders said: *"One has to remember that every failure can be a stepping stone to something better"*. He lived those words, you too should. Become all you can be and get all you can get. Many people are waiting for you to be a blessing to them. Nothing but ALL, you will have to recover in order to become a destiny fulfilled and a joy overflowing. Pray this prayer aloud and aggressively now!

64. *Father, by the power in the name of Jesus and in the blood of Jesus, I recover all that the enemy has stolen from me: my health; my wealth; my joy; my family; my finances; my strength, my career, my*

business, my opportunities, my destiny helpers, my ministry, my fruitfulness, my promotion, my all that I am destined to be. I RECOVER ALL WITHOUT FAIL IN THE NAME OF JESUS!

When troubled times come, be determined to RECOVER ALL. It is a winning key!

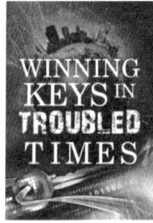

KEY SEVEN

REJOICE ALWAYS

17 Although the fig tree shall not blossom, neither shall fruit be in the vines; the labour of the olive shall fail, and the fields shall yield no meat; the flock shall be cut off from the fold, and there shall be no herd in the stalls: 18 Yet I will rejoice in the LORD, I will joy in the God of my salvation. 19 The LORD God is my strength, and he will make my feet like hinds' feet, and he will make me to walk upon mine high places. Hab 3:17-19 (KJV)

The seventh key for winning in times of trouble is to Rejoice Always. Verse 18 of the above scripture says: *"Yet I will rejoice in the Lord, I will joy in the God of my salvation"*. The moment this man began to do that, troubled times became testimony times.

The truth is that when you shift your focus away from the troubled times and you begin to rejoice in the Lord, the troubles will begin to fight themselves until they are no more. It happened in 2Chro.20. About four nations stronger than Judah came to war against them. The King of Judah, Jehoshaphat called the nation to prayer and fasting. Then God, through a prophet gave them the Winning Key: Rejoice in the Lord, begin to praise and worship Him. As they were praising and rejoicing in the Lord, the bible says the Lord laid ambush against their enemies who began to destroy one another. Not one of the enemy was left after the self destruction. Judah not only won the battle without lifting a finger, they took three days to gather the spoils of their enemies and they still could not finish. The valley of battle became a valley of Blessing for them.

21 And when he had consulted with the people, he appointed singers unto the LORD, and that should praise the beauty of holiness, as they went out before the army, and to say, Praise the LORD; for his mercy endureth for ever. 22 And when they began to sing and to praise, the LORD set ambushments against the children of Ammon, Moab, and mount Seir, which were come against Judah; and they were smitten. 23 For the children of Ammon and Moab stood up against the inhabitants of mount Seir, utterly to slay and destroy them: and when they had made an end of the inhabitants of Seir, every one helped to destroy another. 24 And when Judah came toward the watch tower in the wilderness, they looked unto the multitude, and, behold, they were dead bodies fallen to the earth, and none escaped. 25 And when Jehoshaphat and his people came to take away the spoil of them, they found among them in abundance both riches with the dead bodies, and precious jewels, which they stripped off for themselves, more than they could carry away: and they were three days in gathering of the spoil, it was so much. 26 And on the fourth day they assembled themselves in the valley of Berachah; for there they blessed the LORD: therefore the name of the same place was called, The valley of Berachah, unto this day. 2 Chron 20:21-26 (KJV)

1. *Father, I praise the beauty of Your Holiness. I worship Your Majesty. I proclaim your Most Holy Name.*

2. *I rejoice because I put my trust in the Lord; I shout for joy because the Lord is my defender against every adversary.*

3. *Father, my soul shall be satisfied as with marrow and fatness and my mouth shall praise You with joyful lips in the name of Jesus.*

4. *Father, in prosperity and in adversity, let my joy be constant in the name of Jesus.*

5. *Sing O heavens and be joyful O earth and break forth into singing O mountains; for the Lord hath comforted his people and will have mercy upon his afflicted.*

6. *Father, bring me to your Holy mountain and make me joyful in your house of prayer in Jesus' name.*

7. *Lord, I greatly rejoice in You for you have clothed me with the garments of salvation and covered me with the robe of righteousness.*

8. *Father, give me the supernatural experience of exceeding joy in the midst of tribulation in the name of Jesus.*

9. *Lord as I praise You, turn every valley of battle in my life to that of blessing in the name of Jesus.*

In Phil.4:4 the bible says *"Rejoice in the Lord always; and again I say, Rejoice"* Whatever is repeated twice in scriptures commands particular attention. Rejoicing always in the Lord is an antidote to regrets and regression. 'Always' means at all times irrespective of the situation and circumstance.

> *16 Rejoice evermore. 17 Pray without ceasing. 18 In everything give thanks: for this is the will of God in Christ Jesus concerning you. 1 Thess 5:16-18 (KJV)*

God has promised to deliver you from all troubles but that is when you have done the will of God. It is the will of God that you rejoice and give thanks to God in everything. Do that, and you will experience divine intervention and deliverance.

> *36 For ye have need of patience, that, after ye have done the will of God, ye might receive the promise. Heb 10:36 (KJV)*

To rejoice means to be glad, happy, or delighted; to be full of joy and when you do so in the Lord, you will have dominion over depression and victory over all manners of frustration that troubled times are afflicting you with. Rejoicing in the Lord is a potent and powerful weapon against every adversary. Hear what David said:

> *2 I will be glad and rejoice in thee: I will sing praise to thy name, O thou most High. 3 When mine enemies are turned back, they shall fall and perish at thy presence. Psalms 9:2-3 (KJV)*

The enemies turned back, staggered and died at the presence of the Lord. What provoked the presence of the Lord? The songs of praise of David. The bible says that God inhabits the praises of Israel. Ps.22:3. When praises go up, God shows up and when God shows up, the enemies of his people have no choice but to scatter. I will tell you a true story. Many years ago, my wife was being prepared for a surgery to remove some big fibroids she had in her womb. She reported at the hospital during one of the final appointments preparatory to surgery. While she was waiting to be attended to by the consultant, she just burst into deliberate praise and worship of God. She was rejoicing in the Lord in spite of all the fears and doubts the Doctors have expressed about the surgery. Finally, when the time came to conduct final scans and other medical procedures, the doctors, to their amazement found out that all the big fibroids had disappeared completely. They could not explain what happened. The surgery was cancelled and almost fifteen years after this event, my wife has had nothing to do with fibroid. As you also burst into a moment of rejoicing in the Lord right now, I decree that every plant which my heavenly Father had not planted in you shall be uprooted in the name of Jesus.

You can rejoice in the Lord through many positive attitudes such as singing to the Lord; just praising His name and worshipping God as you are led by the Holy Spirit to do; joyful noise; joyful laughter; clapping your hands; acknowledging God as the 'Winner Man'; rejoicing by confessing the Psalms; dancing to the Lord and by just letting people around you know that there is something different about the way you are always joyful. That way you will be able to tell them the secret of your joy and witness Christ to them. You can also rejoice in the Lord by just giving cheerfully and bountifully.

Ps.126:5-6. 5 They that sow in tears shall reap in joy. 6 He that goeth forth and weepeth, bearing precious seed, shall doubtless come again with rejoicing, bringing his sheaves with him.

James Hudson Taylor said: *"It is the consciousness of the threefold joy of the Lord, His joy in ransoming us, His joy in dwelling within us as our Saviour and Power for fruit bearing and His joy in possessing us, as His Bride and His delight; it is the consciousness of this joy which is our real strength. Our joy in Him may be a fluctuating thing: His joy in us knows no change"*.
I like what Theophane Venard said: *"Be merry, really merry. The life of a true Christian should be a perpetual jubilee, a prelude to the festivals of eternity"*.
You must never forget that true joy is found in Christ. You may not know the Lord and be happy because happiness depends on happenings, but true joy depends on Christ. St. Augustine said: *'There is a joy which is not given to the ungodly, but to those who love Thee for Thine own sake, whose joy Thou Thyself art. And this is the happy life, to rejoice to Thee, for Thee; this is it, and there is no other"*.

When you rejoice in the Lord, you are not denying the troubles. Habbakuk in Hab.3:17-19 did not deny the problem, rather, what you are saying by rejoicing in the Lord is that God is with you in the trouble and because He is bigger than the trouble, the trouble will have to bow to God. Robert Schuller said *"Joy is not*

the absence of suffering. It is the presence of God".
Our Lord Jesus Christ said in Jn.16:33: *"These things I have spoken unto you, that in me ye might have peace. In the world ye shall have tribulation: but be of good cheer; I have overcome the world".*

10. *Father, let no tribulation, distress, suffering, peril or persecution ever separate me from the love of Christ in the name of Jesus.*

11. *I confess that in all these troubles, I am more than conquerors through Him that loves me in the name of Jesus.*

12. *Father, appear in my troubles and let the enemies be scattered in the name of Jesus.*

13. *Father, It is a righteous thing with you to trouble my troublers, arise and do so in the name of Jesus.*

14. *O Lord, send me helpers of joy and make me a helper of joy too in the name of Jesus.*

15. *Adversaries of my soul, what are you waiting for, begin to destroy yourselves in the name of Jesus.*

16. *Father, I praise the beauty of your Holiness. You are the Most High.*

17. *I cast away every garment of shame and sorrow assigned for me in the name of Jesus.*

18. *Let my life be a perpetual Jubilee from now on in the name of Jesus.*
19. *Father, for the rest of my days, give me a crown of beauty for ashes, a joyous blessing instead of mourning, festive praise instead of despair in the name of Jesus.*
20. *Father, shower your blessing that makes rich and adds no sorrow to it upon me in the name of Jesus.*
21. *Henceforth, I decree that sorrow and sighing shall flee away from my life; everlasting joy and gladness shall be my heritage forever in the name of Jesus.*

A brother came to his pastor and told him that he had just lost his job. The pastor replied and said he should give thanks to God. He was puzzled, wondering why the pastor said that. He repeated what he said thinking the pastor did not get his point. "I said, I had just lost my job". The pastor said he heard but that he should still go ahead and thank God that he lost his job and not his LIFE!

Truly, in everything there is always cause to thank God. The elders say that if the slave knows how to think, he will know how to thank. If you want to see a full-tank of blessings, you must be full of thanks to God always. If you want God to raise you; you must always praise Him.

"REJOICE IN THE LORD ALWAYS, and again I say, Rejoice." It is a winning Key in troubled times.

You are a winner. Go ahead and praise God like never before! REJOICE! IT IS YOUR JUBILEE!
God bless you.

OTHER PUBLICATIONS
BY LEKE SANUSI

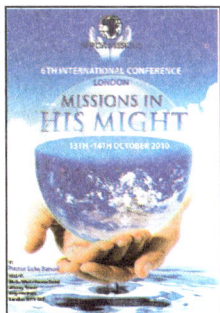
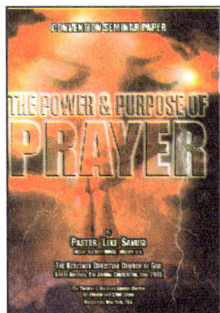
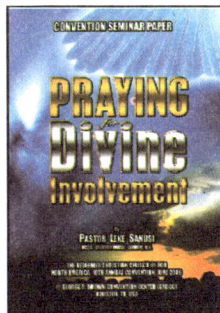
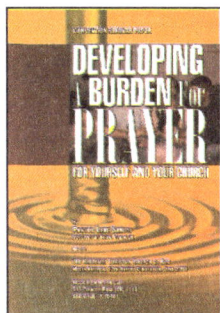
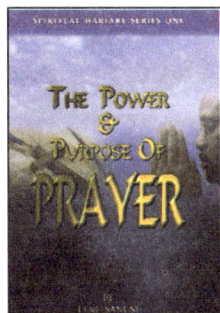
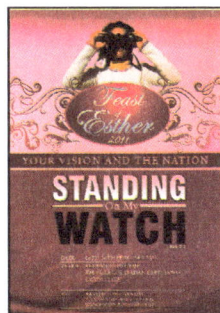
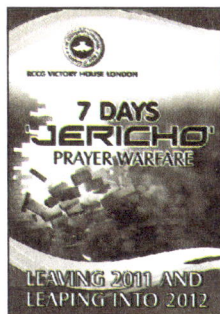
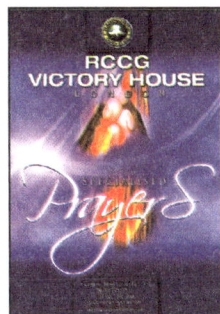
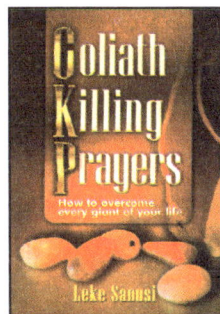
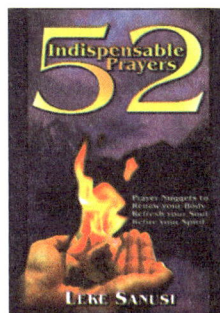
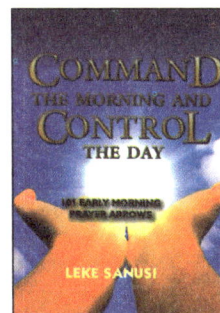

OTHER PUBLICATIONS
BY LEKE SANUSI

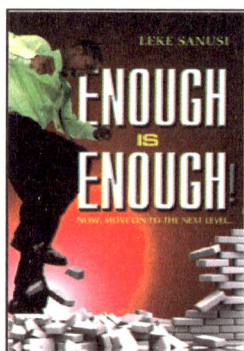

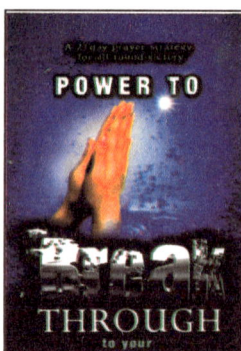

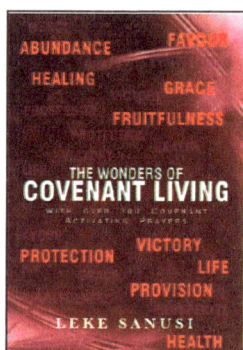

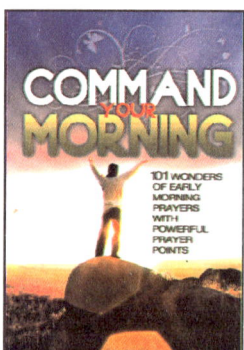

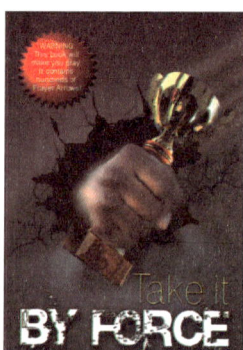